"THE CRYSTAL PALACE IS ON FIRE!"

Memories of the 30th November 1936

GW00707732

by ALISON EDWARDS and KEITH WYNCOLL
Designed by MICK GILBERT

Alison Edwards.

Keith Wyncoll

Acknowledgements

Historical Advice:	Ken Kiss
Additional Material:	Mick Gilbert, Barrie McKay
Research Assistance:	The Crystal Palace Foundation Memories Group, Forest Hill School Oral History Project, Croydon Advertiser, Jean Goodchild.
Photographs:	The Crystal Palace Foundation archives, Anerley Public Library, Patrick Beaver, Marion Blakeman, Alan Burt, Stan Bury, Lionel Crossley, *Daily Mirror*, *Daily Telegraph*, *The Dulwich Wood House*, *Evening Standard* (illustrator: Peter Jackson), John Frost Newspapers, Jean Goodchild, Phyl and Stan Hall, Melvyn Harrison, June Harvey, *The Illustrated London News*, Charles Matthews, The Norwood Society, George Peckham, Patricia Perry, Eric Price, Ken Talbot (*Talbot Collection*), Upper Norwood Public Library.
Lettering:	George Steel
Typesetting:	Words & Pictures Limited, 79 Beulah Road, Thornton Heath, Surrey, CR4 8JG.
Printing:	Cranford Press Limited, 445 Brighton Road, South Croydon, Surrey CR2 6EU.
Publisher:	The Crystal Palace Foundation, 84 Anerley Road, London SE19 2AH.

ISBN 0 9508334 4 4

© The Crystal Palace Foundation 1986

The Crystal Palace, aerial view 1932

"THE CRYSTAL PALACE IS ON FIRE!"
Memories of the 30th November 1936

by ALISON EDWARDS and KEITH WYNCOLL

INTRODUCTION

Fifty years ago, the Crystal Palace at Sydenham was destroyed by fire.

This "people's palace", constructed of iron and glass, had been a centre for "entertainment and enlightenment" for more than eighty years, and as such had been the playground and cultural centre for thousands of people from near and far.

From its dominating position on one of the highest points for miles around, the Crystal Palace was the focal point of life in Norwood for four generations. In the following pages we have attempted not only to relate the story of the biggest peacetime fire this country has ever known, but also to convey something of the people and personalities of the time and how the Crystal Palace and its passing affected their lives.

We are indebted to those who knew and enjoyed the Palace, and who kindly shared their memories with us. Firstly for agreeing to be interviewed by volunteers of the Crystal Palace Foundation's Memories Group, and secondly for allowing some of the tapes to be transcribed here.

Our own text, consisting mainly of background information, appears in heavier type and stands second to the quoted memories of the people themselves who, it is hoped, tell their own story.

ALISON EDWARDS & KEITH WYNCOLL
The Crystal Palace Foundation

CONTENTS

Crystal Palace Parade, 1932

8

"QUICK GIRL, THE PALACE IS ON FIRE!"

Mrs Preece
West Dulwich

"The night the Crystal Palace burnt down I was at home. I'd put my three babies to bed and I was ironing when my husband came in from work; he used to work on shift work. He came in and said, 'Quick girl, the Palace is on fire'. I said, 'Don't be ridiculous, it can't be.' He said, 'Well, you go up to the top of the hill and you'll see it – I'll stay with the children.'

"I went up the road and everybody was rushing up Auckland Hill. The Crystal Palace was one mass of a blaze. You've never seen anything like it in your life – everybody was rushing here and rushing there, cars were blocking the roads. I just stood at the top of the hill and watched, because I had three babies and I didn't want to leave my husband because he hadn't had any dinner.

"I went back and said, 'It's true, dear, it is burnt down.' He said, 'Now what are we going to do? We've got nowhere to go.' So I said, 'Oh, never mind.'"

"We've got nowhere to go" aptly describes the sense of loss which was felt at the destruction of a centre which had been so much a part of South London life for eighty-two years. A whole generation of Londoners under the age of fifty might be forgiven for believing that the Crystal Palace was just a television mast and a Sports Ground. In fact, the original Crystal Palace was that magnificent feat of Victorian achievement built in Hyde Park to house the Exhibition of the Works and Industry of all Nations 1851.

THE YEAR was 1851, and 2000 workmen had completed the Great Exhibition centre in just four months... "The finger of the Almighty," declared one prophet of doom, "will infallibly descend on so presumptuous an enterprise."

The new enlarged Crystal Palace from the Lower Grounds, 1860

PALACE OF THE PEOPLE

The 'Crystal Palace' as it was dubbed by *Punch* was the brain child of the enterprising Joseph Paxton. Head Gardener to the Duke of Devonshire, he indulged his love of conservatories by constructing the Palace on the grandest scale with cast-iron columns, timber glazing bars and a very great deal of glass.

On May 1st 1851, the Great Exhibition was officially opened by Queen Victoria. It housed art and craft treasures from around the world and the best of the Industrial Revolution's new technology and it was an immediate and enormous success. Before it closed in October of the same year, over six million visitors (a figure which was almost equivalent to the total population of England at that time) had come to Hyde Park. Its profits enabled the Exhibition Commissioners to acquire a large part of Kensington on which to build a new centre of art and learning, which eventually included the Victoria and Albert Museum, the Science Museum, the Natural History Museum and the Royal Colleges of Art and Music.

When the Exhibition ended, the newly formed Crystal Palace Company purchased the Crystal Palace from its builders and owners Messrs. Fox and Henderson. It was dismantled, transferred and re-erected at a new permanent location on the crest of Sydenham Hill, South London. Construction of the new building commenced in the early autumn of 1852. The original appearance was altered and an arched nave crowned with three transepts was introduced. The Palace took two years to complete, stretched over a quarter of a mile and at its

highest point reached one hundred and sixty-eight feet. Over one and a half million square feet of glass and nearly ten thousand tons of iron were used in its construction. The building was flanked by two sentinel-like water towers which fed a spectacular array of fountains. Built by Isambard Kingdom Brunel, these were over one hundred feet taller than Nelson's Column in Trafalgar Square and offered a view of seven counties.

The Crystal Palace became a fine recreation centre offering a wide range of 'entertainment and enlightenment'. Its interior was ornamented with works of art, plants, fountains and statues, and a series of courts was built depicting architecture through the ages. It also boasted a concert hall, a theatre and an auditorium that could seat twenty thousand people. Inevitably, Paxton the Palace designer and master gardener landscaped the two hundred acre grounds. Replicas of the world's most famous statues adorned the site, and life-size models of prehistoric animals still thrill the children who visit the park today.

June 10th 1854 saw the opening by Queen Victoria of the Crystal Palace at Sydenham, an event which heralded a new era in leisure, as so many tastes were catered for. People enjoyed archery, rowing, skating, flying, ballooning, soccer, shooting, gymnastics, music festivals, religious and political rallies, fetes, fairs, festivals, exhibitions, firework displays and much more. The Crystal Palace Company also ran schools of art, engineering and physical culture.

Disaster struck in 1866 when the north transept and part of the north wing caught fire and were razed to the ground. Whilst no harm came to the main part of the building, the Crystal Palace Company was unfortunately grossly under-insured and the north transept was never rebuilt, leaving the building unsymmetrical.

In 1911 a vast Festival of Empire was staged. During the Festival, the 'Pageant of London' was performed in the grounds by a cast of hundreds. Despite the Festival's success the upkeep of the Crystal Palace was very expensive and the Official

Osler's Crystal Fountain the focal point of the Nave

Abu Simbel statues, tropical North End

Handel Festival, Centre Transept

Receiver sold the entire property by auction for a mere £230,000. By good fortune, the Earl of Plymouth stepped in and acquired the Palace for the nation. He was refunded by grants from local councils and from money raised by a public appeal launched by the Lord Mayor of London. Under its ownership by the people, a Board of Trustees was formed in 1914, who appointed Henry Buckland as General Manager.

At the outbreak of the First World War the Palace was given over to the Admiralty and became a Naval Training Depot. In 1920, after some restoration, the Palace, housing the new Imperial War Museum, was re-opened by King George V and Queen Mary as the property of the people once more. Happy days returned to the Palace. The famous concerts resumed, plus exhibitions, circuses, dog and cat shows, brass band competitions and sporting events including the introduction of speedway racing. During the thirties the T.V. pioneer John Logie Baird transferred his studios to the Palace.

Mr Peckham
Forest Hill

> *"Inside the Palace it was like Aladdin's cave. There were crafts from various countries – India, China, Egypt, Greece, and beautiful objects made from ivory, inlaid wood and rosewood. As you walked around you thought to yourself, 'I don't know, you're in a different world.' It was really marvellous. When you entered the grounds you came into the Italian terraces which had fountains cascading water."*

Stan Bury
West Norwood

> *"It was like a silver chandelier hanging in the sky when it had a blood red sunset behind it – that was when it looked at its best."*

Bert Slough
Anerley

> *"The toffs had their palaces but this was ours. It was like losing one of the family when it burnt down."*

'PALACE OF THE PEOPLE' was compiled from an article by Barrie McKay

North End fire, 30 December 1866

Festival of Empire, 1911

Dogs on parade, 1933

Watching a firework spectacular, 1935

THE NIGHT THE PALACE BURNT DOWN

'The night the Palace burnt down' is a phrase which sparks off vivid memories for many Londoners. They can often recall their exact movements on the night of 30th November 1936 as others can describe where they were when President Kennedy died.

Mr Goad
Beckenham

"It was a cold and windy night. I looked out of my bedroom window at about eight o'clock (we lived in Forest Hill then, I was ten) and I saw this red glow in the sky. So I called to my brother, 'There's a fire in the next road – let's go and have a look.' So we went out (though we shouldn't have really) and went to the next street, and the next street, and the next street, following the red glow, until we realised that the great Crystal Palace itself was on fire."

Mrs E.M.J. Malone
Croydon

"My mother and I were alone in our house at Highbury Avenue, Thornton Heath. I went upstairs for something and from a bedroom window saw a vivid orange glow in the sky. I called to my mother to come and look and we stood wondering. What could be causing it? It was obviously a big fire and seemed to us then not very far away.

We went outside to the gate but all was quiet and nobody else appeared to have noticed anything unusual. Then a boy cyclist came pedalling round the corner and shouted to us 'The Crystal Palace is on fire!' and off he went. For a moment we were stunned – we couldn't believe it but then we realised the glow was coming from that direction and if it was the Palace, standing as it did on high ground, that would account for the spread of flame being so clearly visible to us."

Gipsy Hill Police Station
Occurrence Book
7.40 pm 30.11.36

A very serious fire occurred at the Crystal Palace, Sydenham; owned by the Crystal Palace Trustees, the General Manager being Sir Henry Buckland who resides at 'Rockhills', West Hill. The fire was discovered by Mr William Charles Ferguson of Kingswood Road, Penge, the staff fireman on duty, who stated:-
'The first I saw was that the ladies' rest room at the rear of the general offices was ablaze. That would be at about twenty minutes to eight. By that time the north end of the rest room was well alight. With staff fireman Clarke we got a hose to bear on it, but realising it was too big for us, I rang the telephone exchange at about 7.50 and asked the girl to call the Fire Brigade. Then Clarke and I continued to play water on the fire until we were forced to leave by the galleries falling. I've no idea what caused it.'

The Palace was almost empty at the time but in the Garden Hall the Crystal Palace Orchestra, conducted by F.W. Holloway, was rehearsing.

B.H. Mathews
Crystal Palace Orchestral Society

"About thirty of our members were engrossed in 'A Tale of Old Japan' when the fire broke out. We did not take much notice when we were told that there was a fire in the Palace, as it was not then considered to be serious. But when Miss Buckland came running in, crying, 'Run for your lives! The Palace is blazing!' we realised how serious things were.

"Once outside the rehearsal room, we could see the extent of the fire. We ran for it. One door was locked, but we went out of another and so reached safety. I can assure you I don't want another experience like that."

F.W. Holloway
Conductor

"The whole of the Handel Festival's Music Library had to be abandoned as well as music by other composers. Original manuscripts worth many thousands of pounds were lost. It was tragic really."

Dorothy Crump
Sydenham

"While we were rehearsing a young girl of about twenty came in and said a slight fire had broken out at the west end, but

there was nothing to worry about. She went away and we went on rehearsing. After I had been playing for a little while, I suddenly remembered that our cars were there and that they might, however small the fire, be in the way of the fire engines. I grabbed my instrument, put on my coat, and started to go out. I opened the door into the main Crystal Palace and shut it again quickly because smoke was very, very bad and the glass was coming down like red hot treacle.

One of the most eerie things was that I heard the most ghastly groans rather like a giant in very great pain. It was only later that I learnt that the noise must have come from the organ. I suppose the heat made the bellows contract and expand and it was like a huge human in terrible pain. It was really rather horrid!"

June Harvey (née Parkin)
Guildford

"My father, a policeman, was on a bus passing the Crystal Palace when he saw flames coming from the building. He stopped the bus and called the Fire Brigade. Then, with the help of the bus crew, managed to push several cars away which were parked nearby and in danger of catching light. He smashed the windscreens of the cars with his truncheon (the truncheon eventually broke) to enable them to be steered to safety.

It was reported that Chrystal Buckland and her father were walking with their dog when Sir Henry noticed a strange red glow in the central transept. He rushed inside and found that the three Crystal Palace Company firemen were fighting a small fire which had broken out in a staff lavatory.

Sir Henry Buckland
Local newspaper report

"Almost within the space of a minute, however, there was a great burst of flame as though there had been an explosion. I saw at once that the situation was serious."

George Norris
Musician

"When I got to the door I looked back to see if anyone was left inside. I could see nothing through the thick wall of smoke, so I slammed the door shut behind me. The Palace was opened by Queen Victoria in 1854 and closed by George Norris on November 30th 1936!"

Police Occurrence Book
The first constable on the scene was P.C. 155Z Parkin who arrived at 7.45 pm, and he called the Penge Brigade. The first brigade to arrive was Penge at 8.03 pm, followed by Beckenham at 8.05. Others followed then at short intervals. The cause of the fire is unknown.

PC 155Z Parkin

Mr White
Tulse Hill

"I had washed some curtains and was putting them back up when I saw a faint haze on the hill. I said to my father, 'I think there must be a fire over Anerley Hill.' So I put my hat and coat on and I went up Anerley Hill to the top of the Parade. The buses were still running, and all I could see was the glow. I went along to the front of the Palace and I could see it was burning inside and there wasn't a fire engine in sight. There were two people walking along to see where the glow was coming from, and while I stood there I suddenly saw the flames begin to creep up the front of the Palace. The orchestra all came dashing out with their instruments and their clothes under their arms. I sat down and watched as all these little flames went up every piece of wood. The glass began to come down, and I thought, 'Oh my goodness, the Palace is on fire', and while I stood there five fire engines came up."

Fireman Stan Bury

'Great Fires and Firemen Past'

At about 19.25 hours, one of the private firemen employed at the Crystal Palace saw a streak of flame run along the top of a room. Quite incredibly, considering the vast risk to the massive building, Penge Fire Brigade was not called until thirty-four minutes later, and when the firemen arrived with their total complement of one motor pumping appliance and eight firemen a severe fire was raging inside the central glazed transept. Despite being hampered in its efforts by crowds of sightsees and motorists, Penge Fire Brigade managed to attack the spreading inferno with its entire resources, one jet of water.

As Penge Fire Brigade, led by Chief Officer Goodman, was only a small force with one slow fire engine, the crew sought help from Chief Officer John Evans at Beckenham Fire Station. He dispatched their new Dennis fire engine. The nine ton 'pump' (ie 'non-escape') engine was a 90 h.p. vehicle – one of only six built for hilly districts.

Second Officer Jameson and his crew of Stan Bury (driver) and Firemen Coupland and Harrison were among the first to reach the Palace – three and a half minutes after the 7.59pm alarm call.

Stan Bury
Fireman

"We were doing 60 mph up Penge High Street. Our first sight of the fire came as we sped up Crystal Palace Park Road."

West Norwood Fire Station received a street alarm call from Farquhar Road at 8.00pm.

New Cross Fire Station received a call at 8.02pm.

The call to West Norwood brought the whole of the London Fire Brigade into action and Chief Officer Goodman (Penge) handed over control to Station Officer Hitchcock of West Norwood.

Report of the London Fire Brigade Committee

On the arrival of the first London Fire Brigade appliances the central transept was well alight and within a few minutes the greater part of it had collapsed. With no dividing walls to resist it and fanned by a strong north-west wind, the fire spread rapidly. The shape of the building was also assisting the spread of the fire, which quickly involved the south transept and threatened to involve the south tower and the adjoining building occupied by Baird Television Limited.

A large crowd of sightseers, increasing by the minute, had collected and gazed with awe and some wonder at how a Palace constructed of iron and glass could burn. The crowd of spectators around the Crystal Palace soon grew to enormous proportions. The BBC Radio News contained the first reports of the fire at 9 o'clock. This brought many people rushing to the scene. Others had seen the glare of the fire which lit up the sky like an exaggerated sunset for miles around, and they followed it as if mesmerized.

A rooftop view of the South Nave

Thronging crowds in Westow Hill

A.G. Bashford
Croydon

> "'That's the Crystal Palace burning', I said to my girl friend as we stood on Windmill Bridge looking along the railway track to the north. Beyond a bank of trees we could see a dense pall of smoke, broken by leaping gushes of flame. 'Don't be daft, lad', said a knowledgeable bystander. 'Glass wouldn't burn like that. It must be a timber yard somewhere'."

H.V. Clarke
Penge

> "It was a beautiful sight but it was wicked – but then, nature is wicked."

'Great Fires and Firemen Past'

> A huge crowd gathered and hampered the efforts of every fresh fire appliance which tried to get to the scene, and once the crews had fought their way through the jostling throng an insufficient water supply added to the problems. The whole of the Crystal Palace area was ankle deep in inter-woven fire hoses, and within an hour of the arrival of the first Penge firemen, over seventy pumps and other appliances crewed by over four hundred fire-fighters were at work."

William Southby
Penge Fire Brigade

> "It was a terrific sight – flames shooting into the sky, and so much molten glass that it looked like a waterfall. We soon realised we would never be able to beat it and had to concentrate on making sure that it did not spread."

Police Occurrence Book

> The fire spread very rapidly and within half an hour the whole Palace was involved – crowds immense and difficult. Aid from adjoining divisions brought in. Crowd of one hundred thousand was estimated by police, vehicular traffic enormous, early diversions but not very effective. Whilst we had no complaints from Fire Brigades, there were delays caused by crowds.

Press
1.12.36

> The traffic as far away as the Oval took on the character of a mad race as pedestrians, motorists, carts all rushed to the Palace.

Mr Morrison
Norwood

"I heard a commotion outside my house on Oxford Road. I parted the curtains and saw people rushing up the road to see where the red glare was coming from. I went out and ran to the top of Roman Road, from where I had many times watched the rockets soar above the transept."

This tragic fire was one of the biggest in peace-time, far more awesome and breathtaking than the spectacular Thursday night Brocks Firework Displays that had thrilled huge crowds, and to which Mr Morrison is referring. Ironically, the Palace's final performance drew one of the largest crowds in its history. A motor car which was parked in Church Road was used as a viewing platform by eager sightseers. It eventually collapsed under the weight, and when the driver returned the front wheels were spreadeagled and the tyres flat.

A.G. Bashford
Croydon

"People had climbed up the trees, and couldn't get down. It was impossible for anyone to move up or down the hill."

Mr Peckham
Forest Hill

"I jumped on my bike and eventually I reached the centre transept. I was foolish to take the bike – it wasn't only a hindrance to myself, it was a hindrance to the firemen. It was really chaotic: the onlookers were stopping the firemen from getting to the fire."

'Fire'
January 1936

Because of the terrific strain on the water supply with so many appliances in action, it soon began to dwindle, and at 9 pm it was impossible, without a vacuum reading on the gauge, to obtain water for the four ¾ inch jets of one of the Beckenham pumps.

Recourse was had to water in an ornamental lake, near the north tower, and by series-pumping effective fire streams were provided for the front of the building.

Albert Stone
Fireman

"My mate and I were hosing down from the roof of a lean-to when the turntable ladder came along, pitched up just where

The South Nave ablaze

we were, and raised the ladder. The fireman called down 'water on'. Of course, the water came on, but it suddenly fell away, stopped. I understood afterwards that the Water Board thought it was a mains burst somewhere, so they shut the water off! When the water came on all of a sudden, me and old Ted Lee were up on the roof. It washed us down! I remember slipping off the top lean-to onto the next lean-to. As I toppled over I could see the ground. I was lucky – I landed on my back. I looked round and saw old Ted beginning to slide down the roof. He couldn't hold on, so I turned and grabbed him! These lean-tos were about six foot high, and I just turned round and grabbed him, stopped him falling."

Police Occurrence Book

A motor car was moved from the centre transept and pushed to safety and also five cars were removed from the Parade near the centre transept.

'The Knoll' owned by Lady Elizabeth Hamilton of 139 College Road, Dulwich, had one hundred yards of oak paling fence damaged by crowds. No 18 Palace Parade had four feet of iron guttering broken by people climbing on roof.

Seven hundred and forty-nine police were kept busy controlling the milling crowds and easing the situation for the firemen. Every available fire appliance from the London Fire Brigade had been summoned, finally totalling ninety engines and five hundred firemen. Many engines were hampered by the onlookers until the police cleared a way to the fire.

Dr G.S. Hislop
Old Coulsdon

"The crowd, the intense activity of fire fighters and police, the roar of the fire, the billowing smoke, and the eerie light over the scene made a vivid and unforgettable impression on me."

Contemporary Press

The crowd, not realising the danger, and thrilled by the spectacle, proved difficult to push back.

Only after the spectators had retreated could hydrants be located and turntables and water pumps put into operation. But despite the numbers of fire fighters and the thousands of tons of water which were poured onto the blaze, the result was negligible. By this time the flames were leaping to a height of

"Everything stops for tea!"

between one hundred and one hundred and fifty feet into the air, and the pressure of water was not sufficient to stem them.

Chrystal Buckland
"The spectators looked on as the immense girders of the Palace twisted grotesquely. The glass buckled and then melted like icicles in the intense heat."

The fire raged until midnight. People left their beds as far away as Brighton, and on ships in the Channel, to gaze at the enormous red glare. Every hill for miles around was packed with people watching the blaze. Field glasses were hired at 'two pence a look' at Hillside Road, Streatham.

Private aeroplanes could be chartered from Croydon Aerodrome at £1 per trip to fly over the Crystal Palace fire. The planes circled at quite a height, but it is reported that the heat of the fire could be plainly felt in the cockpit.

Girders fell throwing up cascades of sparks, and there were constant crashes as the glass fell in. Little by little, sections of the great Palace collapsed.

Mr Peckham
Forest Hill
"Eventually the transept collapsed in front of my eyes and it came down just like a melted lot of lead and glass. It seemed like one colossal fire and that's all you can say about it – flames coming near and glass cracking."

H.V. Clarke
Penge
"It was like a Niagara Falls of molten glass."

Stan Bury
Fireman
"The fireman faced one great wall of flame."

M. Philbert
"It was a very yellow flame. The glass actually caught fire, and when it was really hot there was a sodium flame and the liquid glass was just pouring down."

Albert Stone
Fireman
"Firemen came from all over London. There was also Croydon, Beckenham, and Penge, even from North London. We

were the first appliance up there. We didn't get relieved until one o'clock, when we were told we could go down because the canteen van had arrived. We then had to go back on duty, hosing down. We had to get inside the building. That was when a lot of firemen looked up and got molten glass in their faces. I think there were about six of them taken to hospital.

The Chief Fire Officer of London came up and told us to get out saying, 'Fight it outside!' Because the roof was so high it was a job to reach it with the jets.

Along came our Superintendent. He said, 'What are you doing out here?' We said we were ordered out by the London Fire Brigade. He said, 'Get back in there', so we had to go back in again! A few minutes later the Chief Officer came along again and said, 'Come along, I told you to get out.' I spoke up then and said, 'Our Superintendent told us to get in. Whose orders are we to obey?'

'Obey me', he said. So we had to fight the fire outside, which was right, because it was too dangerous in there."

Police Ocurrence Book

There was one case of personal injury to Fireman H. Freeborn aged thirty-seven of Quinton Street, Earlsfield, who was taken to Norwood Cottage Hospital where he was treated by Dr Starbrook for burns to the face.

Three other firemen were slightly injured – Station Officer Cox and Firemen Stanton and Crutch.

Mrs Ford
Forest Hill

"I was thirteen years of age and was asleep in a little room at the top of the house when I was awakened by lots of noise – people shouting and bells ringing. We lived in a road that was quite close to the main entrance of the park

The flames lit up the sky for miles around

and I wrapped up warm and went outside with my parents. Hot molten glass and metal were flowing down the road and the adults formed a human chain and passed buckets of water from hand to hand in an effort to stem the flow of hot glass."

Mr White
Tulse Hill

"As the glass was melting and running down the gutter on Anerley Hill, people were picking it up and rolling it into balls to keep as souvenirs."

A popular misconception is that molten glass ran down Anerley Hill. However, the facts do not support this as the nearest part of the Palace was over one hundred feet from Anerley Hill.

Mrs Preece

"We saw the flames running along the lead piping. You could see the middle of it cave in – it was a very sad sight really."

Mr Peckham

"Eventually it was all burning, burning . . . people were saying 'Oh, isn't it a shame there won't be another Palace!'"

David Goodchild
Truro

"The chaos and hysterical excitement of the crowd was in the end superseded by a tremendous sense of sadness and shock that such a wonderful centre for sports, the arts, relaxation and pleasure should have burned down."

Robert Cockayne
in the *Star*

"I saw a good part of my own life burning up under my eyes."

Mrs Robinson
South Norwood

"Everybody was crying. It didn't matter who it was. It meant so much to everyone. We couldn't believe that it was never going to be there any more."

Sir Edward Campbell, M.P.

"Everyone must be shocked at the terrible fire which has entirely demolished the Crystal Palace.

"I can imagine and share in the despair of Sir Henry Buckland, the genial and efficient manager, for there can never be a second Crystal Palace as I have known it for more than fifty years.

"As youngsters my brothers and I used to play in the magnificent grounds. We skated on the lakes, when there were several weeks of continuous winter, enjoyed pantomimes, circuses, exhibitions, concerts, and many other entertainments.

"My father, brothers and I played cricket there for the Crystal Palace Cricket Club. In about 1897 this was taken over by the London County Cricket Club, which was run by Dr. W.G. Grace.

"It is all very sad, and as I saw the gigantic blaze from a top window of the House of Commons, I felt a lump in my throat as one has when waving goodbye to one's relations when leaving port on a long voyage."

Mr Morrison
Norwood

"It was a terrible blow to see this wonderful building go."

Contemporary Press

Sir Henry sadly examined the wreck. After the fire was over he spoke to reporters – 'I am heartbroken, my Crystal Palace is finished. There will never be another.'

Chrystal Buckland interjected, 'Cheer up, father, everything will be alright.'

Her optimism was unfounded, however, for although *The Times* had said that it would cost less than a battleship to rebuild the Palace, there was neither the money nor the will to replace Paxton's masterpiece.

Police Occurrence Book

Damage, with the exception of the north and south towers, was confined to the main building which was completely destroyed. Valuation cannot be established. The Baird Television Company of 66 Haymarket, S.W.1. were sub-tenants, occupying a portion of the South Wing which was wholly destroyed. Other buildings within the curtilage were not involved in the conflagration.

At 11.00 pm a message was sent to the Commissioner of Police at New Scotland Yard that no more reserves were required. Main force was dismissed at midnight; by 3.25 am there was still a crowd of five hundred or so left.

Mrs E.M.J. Malone
Croydon

"We felt we had seen enough and the excitement had evaporated as we set out for home, sadly shocked but knowing we had witnessed a little bit of history."

Mrs Ford
Forest Hill

"That once beautiful glass Palace was totally destroyed. The thick smoke was spreading rapidly over the area, and still to this day fifty years on, I remember with sadness the night the Palace burnt down."

The collapse of the South Nave (in sequence, above right)

PYROTECHNICS AT 'THE PALACE'

AT EIGHT O'CLOCK LAST MONDAY EVENING A BRIGHT RED GLOW IN THE CLOUDY SKY BROUGHT ALL SOUTH LONDONERS TO THEIR DOORS AND MANY SURMISES WERE MADE AS TO THE LOCALITY OF THE FIRE . . WHEN THE NEWS REVERBERATED THAT THE CRYSTAL PALACE WAS IN FLAMES THE EXCITEMENT WAS SO INTENSE THAT INFANTS CALLED LOUDLY FOR THEIR SCOOTERS AND INVALIDS ROARED FOR THEIR BATHCHAIRS, SO ANXIOUS WERE THEY TO BE PRESENT AT THE FUN-(PARDON) CATASTROPHE !

"OO-LOOK! IT'S IN GENEVA ROAD"

"'TAINT! IT'S 'ERNE 'ILL !"

"HOOTS MON! UT'S A GRAND SICHT!"

HAMPSTEAD HEATH WAS PACKED WITH SIGHT-SEERS; ALL BRIGHTON SAT UP AND TOOK NOTICE, AND EVERY HILL IN SCOTLAND FROM THE BORDER TO BEN LOMOND WAS INFESTED WITH CANNY SCOTSMEN TRIUMPHANTLY DODGING THE AMUSEMENT TAX, AND

IN THE SWISS ALPS " WONDERING YODELLERS, THINKING TO-MORROW HAD BROKEN OUT IN THE WRONG PLACE, RUSHED HOME AND TOLD THEIR FAMILIES ABOUT IT !

PROVIDED EXCELLENT GRAND STANDS, AND ONE SPECTATOR WAS HEARD TO DECLARE THAT HE WOULD NOT ACCEPT FIVE POUNDS FOR HIS PRECARIOUS PERCH ON TOP OF A CRANE !

THIS SIGHT-SEEING WAS NOT ALL JOY AND GLADNESS, HOWEVER; IT HAD ITS SEAMY AND PATHETIC SIDE . . .

IT WAS A HEARTBREAKING SIGHT TO SEE MIDDLE-AGED GENTLEMEN, WITH THE OUTLINE AND AGILITY OF A HIPPOPOTAMUS, OBSTINATELY TRYING TO CLIMB TREES - SCRAMBLING UP ONE INCH AND SLIPPING DOWN TWO !

ON THE ROOFS OF THE HOUSES WITHIN A MILE OF THE FIRE THERE WAS STANDING ROOM ONLY AT NINE O'CLOCK; THE RAILWAYS

"FIFTY YEARS I'VE KNOWN THE POOR OLD PALACE !"

"(YES-SO HAVE I !"

-HB-

AT ABOUT HALF-PAST NINE A RUMOUR SPREAD THAT THERE MIGHT BE GOLDFISH AND CHIPS FOR SUPPER ! THIS REPORT WAS, HOWEVER, EXAGGERATED . . FIREMEN BUTTED IN AND DISTURBED THE POOR FISH JUST AS THEY WERE GETTING WARM AND COMFORTABLE !

NOW LET US, FOR A MOMENT, BE SERIOUS IF POSSIBLE, AND EXPRESS OUR REGRET THAT THE OLD "PALACE" LIES A MASS OF CHARRED RUINS . . "WHITE ELEPHANT" IT HAS BEEN CALLED, AND WORSE - BUT EVEN "WHITE ELEPHANTS" DO NOT PASS UNMOURNED WHEN THEY ARE HALLOWED BY OLD ASSOCIATIONS AND BY THE THOUGHTS THAT MEMORY BRINGS !

SAVE THE SOUTH TOWER!

The one thought which was in everyone's mind, police, fire fighters and onlookers alike, was "Will the south tower fall?". Certainly there was great danger, for although the wind had veered round to the south-west, the flames still travelled towards the tower. It rose sheer above Anerley Hill, overlooking thickly populated streets, and it was feared that in falling its weight – the top of the tower contained about twelve thousand gallons of water – would cause immense damage and many casualties.

As a precautionary measure, the residents of nearby houses were warned to leave their homes, and many of them found shelter at a local church hall.

Norwood News
4.12.36
> The Rev. C.D. Horsley, Vicar of St. John's, Upper Norwood, went home after watching the fire, and was surprised to find the Parish Hall filled with women and children. He telephoned the police and asked if he should keep the refugees there. The police said that he would be doing a great service if he did, so Mr Horsley made the people comfortable and supplied them with refreshments. He was prepared to keep them as guests all night if necessary, but when word came that the danger of the south tower's collapsing had passed, he was relieved of that task.

Mrs Prince
Anerley Hill
> "Although we were advised to leave the house we did not do so because our daughter was ill in bed. We were thankful afterwards that we did not, but we moved our valuables into the corner of the house farthest away from the tower and hoped for the best."

Mrs Richards
Anerley Hill
> "A very worried-looking policeman came to our door at about 8.30 pm and told us to run for our lives. We had no time to take any of our belongings with us and left the house thinking it was for the last time. An official of the Baird Television Company brought a television receiver into the garden for safety, and for the same reason Mr B.H. Matthews of Snelling's Coal Office, at the top of the hill, brought the office ledgers to the house."

At about 8.45 pm Mr George Metheringham licensee of the Royal Crystal Palace Hotel, was worried of impending danger and advised to clear his premises. Some residents stood on the balcony for a time but soon found it too hot and had to retire.

George Metheringham
Royal Crystal Palace Hotel
> "I didn't leave the premises after the warning. My place was here, and I stayed until I was told there was no danger of the tower's falling down. Then I went out and had a cup of coffee."

Norwood News
4.12.36
> The audience at a cinema in Church Road was informed of the fire and invited to go home, tickets being given to them for another performance.
>
> People living as far away as Waldegrave Road went to bed with their clothes on for fear that the water from the tower would fall and wash their houses away.

Mrs Goddard
Anerley Hill
> "When the order came to get out I had to decide whether to take my puss with me or not. I finally decided that he would be more terrified of the crowds than of anything else, so he stayed where he was. I have been in Norwood all my life and remember the Palace in the old days. I regard the loss as a personal one."

Report of the London Fire Brigade Committee
The efforts were successful, although the fire damaged part of the adjoining building and was only checked within fifteen feet of the tower.

The saving of the south tower was a triumph for the fire fighters and one of the few successes of this fateful night.

SORROWS OF A SPONSOR

MR. PUNCH. "AND TO THINK THAT IT WAS I THAT GAVE YOU YOUR NAME WHEN I WAS A MERE LAD!"

[In 1850, before the Great Exhibition began, Mr. Punch jokingly applied to the Crystal Palace the title which throughout its whole existence it continued to bear.]

Reproduced by kind permission of Punch.

THE AFTERMATH

The next day the glorious palace was a smouldering ruin.

The two gaunt, smoke-blackened water towers (which remarkably were still standing) rose from a twisted mass of iron and great mounds of broken glass. Weary firemen were still hosing down the smouldering remains as hoards of onlookers once more converged on the Crystal Palace on that cold, grey morning.

A few statues were left untouched on the terraces. In the north end of the building bronze statues gazed down on an ornamental fountain in which there were still some goldfish, although their scales had turned completely black. The birds from the Aviary had been released just before the centre transept collapsed and many of them stayed in the Crystal Palace grounds for some days.

Fireman Stan Bury remained on the site for several days damping down the wreckage. To his amazement he found a model Great Western railway engine, which had been operated by a penny in the slot and which had survived intact in its glass case. Virtually nothing else could be saved. The Crystal Palace was no more.

W Thynne
Littlehampton

"I went into the wreckage next morning to recover the large goldfish (which were blue) and take them to the pond by the 'Rotunda'. Within two days they had revived and were golden again."

Albert Stone

"We were up there for three weeks on and off damping down. During that time we had people come up and give us sixpence for a piece of molten glass."

About two hundred Palace employees received their notice the morning after the fire. Some, of them were re-employed to help clear the debris. Part of the Palace was used by Baird employees who were developing television. These workers were also concerned about their jobs.

Frank Rose
Baird Television

"The morning after the fire I went back to the Crystal Palace with my wife. I'd only been married twelve months, and I was

Twisted ruins from the air

worrying as I had just purchased our house on a big mortgage. I saw Captain West the Technical Director, but he told me there was nothing we could do but go home and wait for a week until I received a letter from them. I came home and expected a letter saying this was the end of my job. Lo and behold, the letter came and asked me to report back to duty the following Monday, which I did. The entire staff was met by Captain West, who told us that nobody would lose their jobs. We were all crammed, and when I say crammed I mean crammed, into the School of Arts. We stayed there until 1939, when we obtained new premises at Lower Sydenham, with a brand new factory."

**Norwood News
4.12.36**

Many views are being expressed regarding the future of the site.

Mr Duncan Sandys, MP for Norwood, commenting on the fire, said that while lamenting the passing of an old familiar landmark, he hoped the opportunity would be used to supply the need for a great national sports centre, complete with running track, swimming bath and facilities for every kind of physical exercise. He emphasised the need for a large stadium capable of holding many thousands of spectators to witness displays of physical culture and training.

The Crystal Palace had been an historic monument, he said, and it was therefore fitting that this unequalled site should not merely be used for local needs, but should be utilised to serve a cause of national importance. At the present moment there was a vital need for the provision in London of a centre for the development of physical culture and sport, such as other great capitals already possessed, in order to instil into the British public a proper appreciation of the value to the individual and the nation alike of physical fitness.

Damping down the morning after

Alhambra Court

Remains of the Reno Elevator

Paxton's Tunnel exposed

Sir Henry Buckland sadly gazes at the scene

Investigation

40

ACCIDENT OR ARSON?

Lionel Crossley
Sanderstead

"Just how this great disaster was started is a mystery."

Rumours were soon rife as to the cause of the fire. They ranged from the fanciful to the practical, and none has ever been proved.

Sir Arthur Conan Doyle had earlier resided in the area. Had he been alive at the time of the disaster he would certainly have sent his master sleuth Sherlock Holmes to investigate this burning issue.

Everyone at the time played detective and the 'who-dunnit' debate still occupies many a conversation to this day.

Here we examine some of the theories which then abounded.

A discarded cigarette?

Mr Palmer
Sydenham

"I reckon it was a woman from the Crystal Palace Badminton Club. They played on the night of the fire and after the match they went back into the dressing room where they smoked and then fell asleep. One of the players, I believe she's dead now, all her life said she had a guilty conscience because she felt that one of her cigarettes ......"

He would not complete this accusation when speaking to our volunteer interviewer and records state that the only people in the building at the time were members of the Crystal Palace Orchestra.

H.V. Clarke
Penge

"Well I was talking to a chap this morning, and he was saying, 'You know how the fire was caused?'. 'No', I said, 'even the Fire Brigade won't say.' 'Well', he said, 'You know they had a zoo up there?' 'Oh yes, I remember', I said. 'I could tell you a few stories about that. They used to store all the hay and straw up there, and the big nine inch planks which made up the floor had gaps of about an inch between them. I could see that a cigarette end could have dropped down'."

In fact this gap was only half an inch wide, to aid underfloor heating circulation. Dust fell between the planks and over the years this grew into quite a potentially inflammable layer below the Palace. Another dangerous factor was that the floorboards had become very dry from exposure to the underfloor heating.

Other fire hazards were the vast wooden orchestra area, which could seat choirs of five thousand, and the store underneath which housed twenty thousand wooden chairs, used throughout the grounds in the summer.

Gaps in the floorboards

Destruction by the government?

A very popular view was that the government of the time arranged for the destruction of the Crystal Palace in order to negate the possibility of its being used as a landmark for German bombers on their route into central London during the impending Second World War. It seems unlikely, however, that the Palace would have been destroyed so early, as war was yet three years away.

Another factor against this theory is that iron from the devastated Palace was sold as scrap to Krupps, the industrialists who fed the German war machine. It seems unlikely that this sale would have been allowed to take place had war been so strongly expected. Ironically, some of the original Palace iron may have returned to London in the form of bombs.

An insurance swindle?

Lionel Crossley
> *"From 1927 until 1934 the Palace had enjoyed halcyon years, when enormous crowds passed through the turnstiles to watch motor-cycle racing, speedway, boxing, wrestling, tennis and other tournaments, and the Bank Holiday extravaganzas which attracted upwards of 100,000 patrons. The rents and rates for all these sporting functions were annually increased to such an extent that in 1934 the speedway promoters moved to New Cross."*

In spite of this loss of revenue the Palace still made enough money to employ sixty-four window cleaners, dozens of gardeners and groundsmen, cleaners, office staff, etc.

Lionel Crossley
> *"Why did Lloyds pay out £120,000 in compensation after a very sparse investigation? This represents about £5,000,000 in today's money."*

Contrary to rumours of an insurance swindle the building (at £110,000) and Great Organ (£10,000) were perhaps undervalued and therefore under-insured at the time of the fire. Lloyds made a straightforward payout due to a "total loss through fire".

It was a sign of the times that the building, having cost £1.3 million to build, was valued at only £200,000 when sold in 1911.

Did Sir Henry Buckland set light to his own Palace?

This popular theory seems unlikely in light of the above. Also, the Palace staff knew that he was so devoted to his life's work that this would be unthinkable.

Bert Slough
Anerley
> *"I stood by Sir Henry Buckland. He was in tears as he watched the devastation of his twenty-five years' work."*

Sabotage by disgruntled workmen?

Barrie McKay
The Crystal Palace Foundation
> *"It is said that Sir Henry was very unpopular for being a hard task master – some people have even suggested he had to wear a hat all the time for fear of having things dropped on him by workmen on roofs."*

H.V. Clarke
Penge
> *"He came along one morning, all dressed up in his grey topper and tails with his silver-mounted walking stick and he said, 'Good morning'. We just turned around and said, 'Good morning'. He said, 'Don't you know who I am?' Well, we weren't interested. So he said, 'I am Sir Henry James Buckland, General Manager!' I wouldn't like to repeat what the other people working with me said!"*

Workmen would have had access to where the fire started but would have been unlikely to have wanted to destroy their workplace and livelihood (see *The Aftermath*).

Split gas cylinders

A gas leak, or a gas explosion?

Mrs Maynard
> *"I heard an explosion and the flames shot in the air."*

Newspaper comments also mentioned hearing several loud explosions at about 9 o'clock. This coincides with the fire reaching Baird's Television Studios where a number of oxyacetylene cylinders were stored. These later were found split open by the explosive force of the gas being overheated by the fire. As this was long after the fire had started it could not have been the cause of the disaster.

Neither is there any evidence to suggest that the 'town's gas' supplied from Sydenham Gas Works played any part in starting the fire. If there had been a gas leak prior to the fire this would have been smelt by the Palace staff. Had there been a major leak and then a fire is is almost certain that an explosion of some magnitude would have demolished most of the building in seconds.

A member of the Palace staff reported seeing "blue flames" which were probably caused by the burning asphalt that had been laid over the wooden floors.

Albert Stone
Fireman
> *"I was hosing down when I saw these two men on the ground going towards the gas main. I found out later that the Gas Company had dug a trench six foot long and got down to this gas pipe which I understood to be a twelve inch main, and they cut one end off the pipe and stuck a pig's bladder up. So they cut out the gas, and what gas there was in the remainder of the building burnt out. A policeman told me later that it took them only half an hour to dig that trench."*

A fault in the heating?

Mrs Garston
Forest Hill
> *"The heating in the Palace went wrong and the resulting combustion started the fire. The metal melted, the wind caught the fire, and whoosh!"*

There is no evidence to support this theory.

Undamaged gas meter

An electrical fault?

H.S. Benbow
Orpington

"I went with a host of Sunday Schools to sing our songs at the Palace. Children drawn from all over the country took part. During the last rehearsal we had, my friend and I remarked about the narrow passages lined with tinder-dry shelves laden with bills and papers of all sorts. Electric wires just rested on them, with lamps every so often to light our way under the staging to get to our seats. We were both alarmed at what we saw and said, 'What if this lot caught fire!' "

Certainly many people feel that poorly insulated wiring shorting onto the dry timber framing, somewhere in the centre of the building, could have been the cause of this disastrous fire.

Barrie McKay

"The Crystal Palace Foundation's consensus of opinion is that it was probably an electrical fault which started the fire. The Palace was one of the first large public buildings to be installed with electricity and some of this wiring was probably quite old and ineffectively insulated. However, after all our researches we are still very much aware that this is only conjecture and the cause of the fire remains an open question."

Searching the remains.

The ruins,
a tanged mass of ironwork

THE END OF AN ERA

Gordon Savage
New Addington

"There never has been, never will be, another Entertainment Centre like Prince Albert's fantasy."

The Star
1936

It had been difficult to heat in winter, impossible to cool in summer, oddly shaped and too big, but to Londoners it was the symbol of a great past, and of happy days that they would never forget.

On 30th November 1936, an era in London's history came to a close.

The heart was ripped out of South London, but dramatic as the fire was, its significance fades when one's thoughts return to the heyday of the Crystal Palace, the "playground for millions".

The spirit of Crystal Palace lives on in the efforts of the Crystal Palace Foundation and in the minds of those to whom it meant so much.

APPENDIX 1 – FACTS & FIGURES

DIMENSIONS

Length of Nave	1,608 ft
(after 1866 fire)	1,392 ft
Width of Nave	72 ft
Height of Nave	104 ft
Length of each Wing	576 ft
Width of Central Transept	120 ft
Length of Central Transept	384 ft
Height of Central Transept	168 ft
Width of North & South Transepts	72 ft
Length of North & South Transepts	336 ft
Height of North & South Transepts	104 ft
Height of North & South Tower	275 ft
Weight of Iron	9,642 tons
Area of Glass	1,650,000 sq ft
Weight of Glass	500 tons
Number of Bricks used	6,156,000
(enough to build 126 houses)	
Amount of Wood	75,000 cu ft
Total Area of Main Building	603,072 sq ft

WEATHER

Forecast at 6 pm, Croydon, 30th November 1936:

Barometric Pressure	1013.4 falling
Wind Direction	WNW changeable
Wind Speed	Force 5 (10–24 mph)
Temperature	50°F
Humidity	65%
Visibility	6 moderate visibility 6½ miles
Cloud Form	Low layer of stratus or stratus-cumulus
Amount of Cloud	Overcast sky with a few small traces of low cloud
Cloud Base	5,700 feet
State of Ground	Wet

Upper Norwood Fire Brigade 1860s

FIRE BRIGADE

The first call was received by Penge at 7.59 pm.
The first appliance was on the scene at 8.03 pm.
In all, 88 appliances and 438 officers and men were employed.

Penge Brigade: 1 motor pump, 1 officer, 8 men.
Beckenham Brigade: 2 motor pumps, 1 motor tender, 2 officers, 11 men.
Croydon Brigade: 1 motor pump, turntable ladder with pump, 1 officer, 11 men.
London Brigade: 61 motor pumps, 4 turntable ladders, 2 tenders, 2 emergency tenders, 9 lorries, 1 canteen van, 7 officers, 374 men.
London Salvage Corps: 3 tenders, 2 officers, 21 men.

The seat of the fire probably reached a temperature of 2,000°F
The cost of the Brigade's attendance was £2,666-0-6d.

POLICE

The first Police Constable on the scene was PC155Z Parkin.

749 police were deployed as follows:-

1 Superintendent
2 Chief Inspectors
7 Senior Divisional Inspectors
21 Inspectors
62 Sergeants
651 Constables
5 Mounted Police

Keeping the sightseers back

THE GLOW OF A SUNSET WHICH REFUSED TO FADE AROUND LONDON ...

Banstead: (8 miles) "It was as though giant rockets were being fired and great pillars of sparks could be seen."

Biggin Hill: (8 miles) "It was like a huge scarlet bonfire. Flames could be distinguished as well as a vague outline of hills and houses."

Vincent Square, Westminster: (8 miles): every balcony was crowded and people climbed on to the roofs to get a better view.

Hampstead: (12 miles) "Tongues of flame shot from the crumbling roof, lighting the sky."

Parliament Hill Fields: (12 miles) householders attracted by the glare rushed out to open ground.

Sevenoaks: (15 miles): "A fierce reddish light."

Enfield: (17 miles): the movement of flames was visible.

AND FURTHER AFIELD.

Cheshunt: (20 miles): "The red glow stretched across the sky."

Iver, Buckinghamshire: (25 miles): the fierce glow could be clearly distinguished.

Hindhead: (39 miles): hundreds of people gathered at the Gibbet, where a glow in the sky reflecting the destructive flames could be seen.

View from a plane

Brighton: (50 miles): the flames could be seen as a dull red glare. Scores of people in cars watched the phenomenon, which appeared like the glow of a sunset which refused to fade.

Mid Channel: (80 miles): the pilot of an Imperial Airways plane flying at 7,000 ft could see the blaze.

49

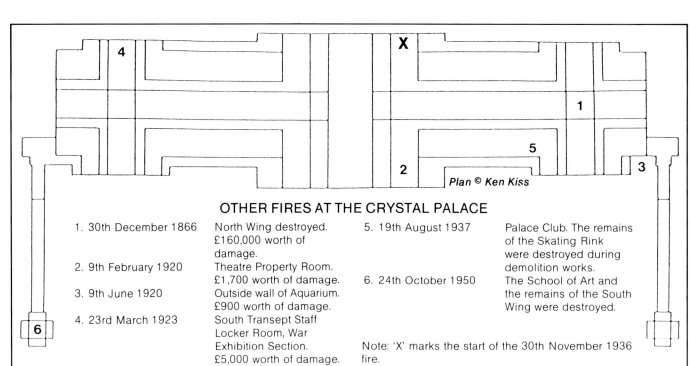

OTHER FIRES AT THE CRYSTAL PALACE

1. 30th December 1866 — North Wing destroyed. £160,000 worth of damage.

2. 9th February 1920 — Theatre Property Room. £1,700 worth of damage.

3. 9th June 1920 — Outside wall of Aquarium. £900 worth of damage.

4. 23rd March 1923 — South Transept Staff Locker Room, War Exhibition Section. £5,000 worth of damage.

5. 19th August 1937 — Palace Club. The remains of the Skating Rink were destroyed during demolition works.

6. 24th October 1950 — The School of Art and the remains of the South Wing were destroyed.

Note: 'X' marks the start of the 30th November 1936 fire.

Crystal Palace Fire Station 1904

APPENDIX 2 – BBC RADIO BROADCAST

This is a transcription of the commentary broadcast at approximately 9.45pm on Monday 30 November 1936 on the occasion of the Crystal Palace fire. The commentator was standing on the flat roof of one of the row of lock-up shops between Farquhar Road and Westow Hill.

The following British Broadcasting Corporation staff were on duty:
S.J. de Lotbiniere *Commentator, Head of Outside Broadcasting*
R. Murray *Second Commentator*
Robert Wood *Engineer*
Mr Crouch *Senior Assistant Engineer*

First Commentator:
The wind is blowing from the west straight across, and the whole of the centre parts have come down. I've got the wind coming over my head from the back blowing away from London and *that* a little while ago looked pretty hopeful.

They've got the fire under control. They've been moving fire engines for the last few minutes taking them to the north and the south so as to get going with the towers. Another little fire seems to have broken out on the building just below the south tower, but I rather think that there's a fair gap in between and it looks to me as though they'll probably get that under control and save the south tower. The south tower's the one where the Baird television works are, and we'd hoped originally to link our lines up there so as to be able to talk to you from here, but as soon as we arrived we saw there was no question of that, nobody could go there unless they'd got a fireman with them and occasionally one saw a light go up. There must be a spiral staircase inside, and through the glass one saw this light going up and up and up, but at the moment it looks deserted and I should think they're keeping people well away.

Further along at the north tower I can see it almost for the first time because the smoke has cleared. Unfortunately it looks as though the fire's spreading a bit towards the north nave.

It is ablaze and all the while you see coming down molten bits of metal and glass like a firework display. In fact, it sounds a bit cruel to say it but I doubt if they've ever staged a better firework display here than they have tonight.

View from Farquhar Road showing BBC commentators on shop roof

I should think that the whole steel framework of that north nave may collapse at any moment and I don't know how it'll affect the tower beyond, possibly they've been able to clear away any structure below so that the thing won't spread.

Doesn't look to me as though there's any hope of rain coming from anywhere, it's a pretty clear sky and a moment ago there was almost a full moon looking straight at me across this blaze of smoke and ruins. Looking into the building you can see twisted girders and some of those pillars that a lot of us knew when we went to visit the Crystal Palace. The organ and the whole of that central hall's on the ground now smouldering and burning and the occasional bit of wind catches it and makes the flames fly up again.

There's a fairly strong wind. I'm up on the top of a house here, and somebody has got an umbrella behind me trying to shield the microphone. I don't quite know how much of the wind on the microphone you may be getting, but I hope you can hear what I'm saying.

On the whole the crowd've cleared off by now. A little while ago, there was an enormous crowd all round and the police were keeping them back and pushing them down the side roads which had quite a lot of cars in, but with this cold wind they've begun to clear off.

The Croydon Aerodrome people have evidently been doing a trade giving people a view from the air because we had a lot of aeroplanes over here a moment ago, but I expect the've gone back to put down their passengers and they'll be coming again with their navigation lights showing.

I believe by the north tower they've pretty well drained the boat pool with the water they've used for the pumps but I should think they may be having a bit of a difficulty. We're high up here looking right back over London and right on the other way over Beckenham, and I should think that means that the water pressure's none too good.

The smoke's going right away from me so I can see the whole length of this blazing mass but the people Beckenham way probably can simply see a pall of pale pink smoke. When I started out at nine from north London I could see a bit of a pink glow, then I crossed to the river at Vauxhall bridge. I knew my way to the Crystal Palace alright but I didn't have to look at roads or anything, I could see this great glow in the sky and I just drove straight for it. By the time I got to Camberwell Green I didn't have to even look at that because there were people hurrying everywhere, cars driving as hard as they could go and the pavements packed with people hurrying towards the fire, and by the time I got here there was a large crowd. I should think they must have had most of the fire engines in London here but just here halfway between the two towers they've

cleared off now and apart from the occasional fireman who I suppose is on duty keeping an eye on things one doesn't see many.

The building just between me and the south tower is beginning to blaze up and I can see smoke coming through all tiles on the roof and flames shooting out of the four chimneys, but I should think that even if that does go . . . What! – they tell me there's something wrong about my position by the microphone. I must find out. There's a Dickens of a lot of wind on the microphone but I don't quite know what I do, hold on a minute. I'll try and open my coat and see if that'll protect it. Not that there's a great deal more to tell you unless I keep you here all night because the principal excitment will be this north nave. It's still blazing all over the whole framework and I can't believe that it'll hold. I think there will come a moment when the whole thing'll crash and there'll be the most amazing shoot up of flames and sparks but I don't know if it's much good keeping you up to hear about that. I think the only thing to say is that so far as I know and I haven't bothered the experts because it seems to me on an occasion of this sort . . . Hello, here is an expert.

Second Commentator

Not at all an expert but I've just come round from behind the other side of the building right in the gardens and it's on the leeside where all the smoke's being blown across. It's a most extraordinary sight. You can see the great building right up above you , and the wind is blowing huge clouds of acrid smoke right across and sparks that are travelling a matter of two hundred yards and there's glass all over the grass and those strange shrouded females that inhabit the parks are being peppered with flying sparks and flying glass.

Down by the pond where the motor boat racing or the motor boat sport takes place there are about twenty pumps all going for all they're worth, and the pumps at the south end are being transferred now down there because this end is more or less under control, whereas that is quite definitely still blazing furiously.

Right round the building there are a matter of half a dozen hoses shooting up over into the leeside of the building, that is into the lower part of the north transept. They're still directing jets hoping to check something, but the spray's being blown back as much as it's blowing being directed right into the building, and one gets exceedingly wet trotting round there in the grass.

There's nothing very much more to tell except that it's burning and burning and burning. Right down on the other side close by where the pumps are stationed there's a fire brigade canteen. The men are queueing up already and taking what looks like meat pies and hot tea and coffee. More engines are even now being transferred by the looks of it from this end right under the lee of the tower to the north nave. Of course the middle of the building is absolutely flat as your hat.

First Commentator

Well I don't know if there's really much more to say. I'm told that the first part of the broadcast was probably missed. I might as well explain to you that this was just fixed up at very short notice. We're on the top of a roof on the west terrace of the Crystal Palace looking down the whole length of the burning girders and glass, the south tower on our right and the north tower on our left. We just rigged the thing up quickly and I don't suppose you're getting very good quality with this wind blowing on the mike but it's the best we can do. The north nave that I was telling you about is still smouldering away. There looks to me as though there's a good deal less flame, and that may mean that the thing may hold up and not collapse. No doubt between that and the tower they've got rid of any buildings that might carry the flames on to the north tower and I expect they'll save it, and I should say probably the same with the south tower. So, let's ... Oh there's something more to be said.

Second Commentator

Just let me tell you one more story and that is of the south wing which leads down to the low level railway by a long and rather complicated sub-

way. In the lower part of it, as those of you who have been here may remember, are all sorts of those shrouded females and vast statues there waiting in the dark to be burnt. The flames are moving at the rate of about a yard in every five minutes and the roof is coming crashing down in sections. A good dozen hoses inside and outside are squirting away for all they're worth. The whole lining of that corridor is matchwood and the fire was eating along that at a terrific pace. Even now there's quite a considerable blaze on the roof of the building right under the tower against which the fight has been raging all the evening.

First Commentator

Well I think that's about the end. I can see a lot of cars piling up in the road. This building where we are has a drop of about fifty foot behind onto the Southern Railway line. I can see looking down a road a lot of cars which must be the West End crowd arriving after the West End shows.

Well, I don't think we can keep you here any longer. I s'pose this'll go on blowing through the night. There'll be policemen here on duty all night and there'll be the firemen working. Let's hope they get through with the least possible damage to themselves, and let's hope they save the two towers. So we'll now leave the Crystal Palace and go back to Broadcasting House.

Reproduced with kind permission of the BBC.

The Crystal Palace cat

The following evocative letter was written the day after the fire by a Baird employee to his fiancée in Lancashire. He was anxious to reassure her that despite the fire his employment was safe so their future together was secure.

Tom Nuttall
Chelmsford

"Elsie Dear

I am on holiday today so I can write to you without wondering all the time whether I shall catch the post.

I expect the account I gave you yesterday was rather incoherent so I will try to tell you again what has happened.

We had all finished work at about 6.30 and I had my tea as usual. At about 8 o'clock someone shouted down the stairs to say there was a big fire on. I looked out and saw the sky lit up, so I went out to investigate. It gave me a horrible feeling to realise that the Palace was burning.

At that time the fire was localised on the far side of the centre transept, so our part of the building was quite clear. The door was locked and the doorkeeper was somewhere in the building, so somebody climbed over the gate to open the door. When we got in everything looked quite normal and we could walk the full length of our corridor. Towards the end of the corridor it was beginning to get hot from the fire above.

We opened the emergency doors in case we had to make a sudden departure and then proceeded to remove some of the more dangerous things such as gas cylinders and flasks of liquid air which would have exploded in the fire.

We removed such papers and letters as we could lay our hands on and a few small valuable pieces of apparatus, but there were not enough of us to attempt to remove any of the larger things. The studio cat was rescued. Eventually the firemen ordered everybody to leave the premises as, although our section still appeared quite safe, there was a slight danger of some of the upper parts of the structure falling in on to our side.

I took a last look down the corridor before leaving. The colour scheme of the decoration was yellow and red, all the walls and ceiling being a creamy yellow colour and the doors a soft red to tone with the walls. The clocks were going, and looking down the corridor one would have thought that everything was quite normal except that towards the far end it appeared to be slightly foggy as the smoke was beginning to leak in.

Although the fire started in quite a small area, the firemen were unable to prevent it spreading and it was quickly realised that the whole of the building would have to burn itself out. It was terrible to feel so helpless. We knew that these premises, still looking spick and span and containing so much of our work, would soon be nothing but a pile of rubbish and there was nothing at all we could do to prevent it.

I could not bear to watch it burning so I left. By this time the streets were packed with sightseers and I had to use brute force to get through the crowds. All traffic was stopped except for police cars and fire engines and the police had brought a loud speaker car to direct the crowds. Thousands of cyclists had turned up and they and their machines were jammed together unable to move at all except for a few of the taller ones who were able to carry their machines over their heads.

I thought you might hear about the fire and become anxious so I wanted to telephone to reassure you. When I got in sight of the telephone box I found it was besieged and I could not get near. Eventually I was able to make my way to the cafe where I have lunch. The proprietress recognised me and took me through to their house to use their telephone. Before leaving I had a coffee with one of our fellows who stays there.

The glare from the fire was terrific. Several aeroplanes were circling round taking photos and news reels and there were also some air liners. Being nightime, they were carrying red and white lights, giving the appearance of a huge firework display round a bonfire.

When I got back, Westow Street had been turned into a car park for sightseers. Visitors parked their cars here and walked the rest of the way.

Miss Payne was very upset, partly because she has known the Crystal Palace since she was a girl and partly at the thought of losing her circus lodgers. I will not assess the relative importance of the two parts. She had been drinking and was almost hysterical. She came into my room about 10.55 and nearly made me miss the post. She had a bad night and did not waken till 9 o'clock this morning. I went to bed soon after midnight but did not get to sleep till after 2 o'clock with the worry and the noise and the cars and the aeroplanes.

This morning I went to find out what the position was. The firemen were still in possession and we were not allowed to enter. We were told to report for duty tomorrow.

I met some of the other fellows and we looked round the outside of the building and then had coffee. I was able to obtain details from a man who had been in attendance till 2 o'clock. The whole of the main building, containing most of our labs, has been destroyed. It was feared at one time that the fire might reach the south tower, and all the houses in Anerley Hill were evacuated in case the tower (300 feet of it) should collapse. Parts of the main building were dynamited to cut off the advance of the fire and the tower was saved. A small building, near the foot of the tower, which also contained apparatus, was likewise saved.

Our receiving set production is carried out in a separate building, near the foot of the tower, reached by a long passageway. It was found possible to cut off the advance of the fire in this direction so that the building was saved and production is going on normally today. This is very fortunate financially as we derive a considerable profit from the sale of receiving sets. The only snag here is that the cathode ray tubes used in the receivers were made in the main building where all the plant has been destroyed. We have, however, a considerable stock of these tubes, and we hope to be able to start production again before the stock is exhausted.

As regards the experimental work we shall not know the full position until we have had a meeting tomorrow when we shall be able to decide on a plan of action. The most unfortunate aspect is the delay which has been caused in our programme, for it will take us some considerable time to replace the lost equipment. I think we shall be able to find suitable accommodation and we shall probably have to start by doing such elementary jobs as fitting up tables and benches to work on. Everybody seems quite cheerful, and if we all pull together the position is not hopeless. The traffic is very dense today and it is moving slowly. There are still crowds of people on the pavements. At the roundabout there is a policeman on each of the four roads and the loud speaker is giving instructions to the traffic and stopping it occasionally to let pedestrians cross.

The aeroplanes have been swarming round all day like vultures round a corpse. Several RAF machines have chased them away from time to time but they keep returning. I have heard that one of the planes nearly had an accident last night. It got caught in the hot air current from the fire. The pilot lost control and side slipped missing the south tower by a few feet. Fortunately the steep hill gave him a little extra height in which to regain control, otherwise he would probably have crashed.

There was a salvage corps with some ambulances here, but I have not heard of any casualties apart from several women who fainted in the crowd.

I am terribly sorry that our future happiness should have been threatened by this fire, but there is no cause for despair. Baird Television is not finished yet. With sufficient determination we should still win through.

Don't forget to see Sylvia Sidney in 'Fury'.

Love Tom"

Summer 1937

THE CRYSTAL PALACE FOUNDATION

Fifty years on we examine what has happened to the Palace site and what is planned for its future:–

The grounds have become one of London's premier parks with recreational and entertainment facilities still enjoyed by large numbers of people. The centre of the park now houses the National Sports Centre with a stadium and indoor sports complex. These are on the site of the two massive grand fountain basins that were later used for football, then as a speedway stadium with an adjoining cycle track. All this is in the lower 150 acre grounds; the top 50 acres where the Crystal Palace itself stood have lain largely derelict since the fire.

The two Brunel water towers were demolished during the war which also saw the Italian Terrace used as a vast car breakers' yard to feed the munitions factories. In the 1950s the television transmitting station arrived and most of the statues departed – sold off to grace places as diverse as Bing Crosby's estate and blocks of flats in South London.

Several grand plans were proposed for this magnificent hilltop site but all were dismissed as impractical or too expensive.

However, on a cold wet May day in 1979, half a dozen local enthusiasts held a small exhibition about the history of the Crystal Palace. They were completely overwhelmed by the 1,000 people who came to the event. These were a mixture of those who had previously enjoyed the Palace and younger people keen to discover about the history of the area.

The Crystal Palace Foundation was formed later that year as a charitable voluntary organisation concerned to promote the memory of the Crystal Palace and to enhance the public amenities of the site and its historic connections. The 1,300 CPF members are engaged in:

a) establishing a Crystal Palace Museum,
b) undertaking restoration of the terraces,
c) promoting education and research including publishing work about the Palace,
d) organising exhibitions, guided walkabout tours, discussions and other events reflecting the importance of the Crystal Palace in our history.

From this practical experience, the Foundation compiled proposals outlining their "CRYSTAL PALACE MUSEUM AND PARK RESTORATION PROJECT". These were adopted by the Greater London Council in 1981 who then began to skilfully restore the terraces. Following the abolition of the GLC, Bromley Council are keen to support the CPF aims and they are currently preparing a landscape master plan to improve the whole park.

The CPF is actively encouraging people who visited the Palace to share their memories by letter or through taped interviews. These fascinating accounts are often published in "CRYSTAL PALACE MATTERS", a quarterly magazine that is sent to Foundation members and sold in local newsagents and bookshops.

Today the Foundation has emerged as the leading authority on the Palace and has acquired a large archive, to be displayed in the eagerly awaited Crystal Palace Museum. The former Palace School of Engineering building, by the base of Brunel's south water tower, is being converted to house the first phase of the museum. At the time of writing, the CPF Museum Appeal is halfway to raising the amount needed to open this centre in 1987.

If you are interested in receiving more information about the Crystal Palace Foundation, please contact: Eric Price, CPF, 84 Anerley Road, London SE19 2AH. Tel: 01-778 2173.

Other publications by CPF include *Crystal Palace Speedway* (£3.95) and *Fire!*, produced in conjunction with the Croydon Advertiser (95p).

Crystal Palace Museum building

58